From My Holographic Heart to Yours

Notes for the Evolving Soul

Take your desires seriously.
To long for
is to have known.

It has not been mindless
to be born in the aching
arms of Nostalgia,
to reach through every
darkness for you.

In the beginning the Universe was smaller than the smallest you have ever felt, and look at how big it's grown, look at all the reasons to believe in you.

It is the pathologization of sensitivity that creates pathological sensitivities.

The heart's electromagnetic field is even bigger than the brain's, so it's not only romantic to follow your heart but scientific and smart.

When you give up trying to be understood by others you surrender to being understood by yourself.

We are channels for the Source energy from which we all come. We are Divine instruments of Love.

You have known your home otherwise you would not long for it.

There is only one path
and it is yours.

We are not the pain we have carried.

A person may experience mental dis-ease – a lack of ease in the mind – but to call this experienced "a diseased mind" is a violation of their soul.

God does not speak *to* us but *through* us. God is the movement we are.

You weren't supposed to "fit in" otherwise you would have. You fit in perfectly with the evolutionary expansion of the Universe.

A scientific fact is that pain cannot last forever.

Part of the healing process includes allowing yourself breaks even from that process.

We are the Universe expressing itself so there would be a way for the Universe to know itself.

The stars don't know they are stars and so they might as well not be stars. We know that we are so that we could be. We exist so that wonder could exist. We exist so that Love could exist.

You are the miracle that allows for miracles to exist.

The Universe expresses itself to you through symbols and signs in order to respect your free will in deciding whether or not to pay attention to those signs. The Universe will never force you. There is no force in Unconditional Love. Only acceptance. And more Love.

The Universe loves you so much it will respect your autonomy in all ways, even in the choice to not love yourself. It believes and honors your power that much.

Humans are not God but we are not only humans. Humanity is a vehicle for the expression and evolution of God, which is to say, ourselves.

Scientists searching for God will find God when they realize their desire to find God *is God*.

To feel is Divine.

Science as we currently know it will never prove the existence of God because to search for God outside the self is to deny God.

To fundamentally change the world we must change the foundation from which the world is experienced: our consciousness.

We are nature with the
awareness of being nature.
Your thoughts are seeds.
Your subconscious is the soil.
What you plant will grow.

To build Heaven in the world you must first build Heaven within you, remember the Heaven that you are.

The process of my being is my being. My person is the expression of the process that I am.

Together we really can build a better tomorrow, but we cannot be together until we are with ourselves.

The future is the energetic vibration of the present. When you consciously live in the present you are able to consciously create the future.

Your consciousness is God, creator of all. To believe in someone is to give them the power of your consciousness, the gift of God.

You are who you are today because of who you believed you were yesterday.

Divine Love is the Divine Order.

The person most deserving of your empathy is you.

We've been conditioned to scoff at the power of prayer because of the pathologization of the feminine energy of intuition.

Prayer is as powerful as you believe it to be.

To intentionally pray is to access and shape energy in higher-dimensions, which will then manifest in our waking reality in Divine timing.

Infinite potential is your natural state. Tune into your preferred frequencies. You are your favorite possibility.

Let go of everything you think you know so that all you may know is Love.

Live not as if you're dying but as if you're already in Heaven.

Just because you can feel everybody else's feelings doesn't mean you have to.

All souls go to Heaven because all souls came from Heaven. It's just a matter of time i.e. the 4th dimension i.e. which version of you are you tuned into?

The truth often feels like a lie at first because we've absorbed so many lies as the truth.

When others don't accept positive changes within you it's only because they're not ready to accept positive change within themselves. They can't believe you're real because they can't believe they are.

When we live in fear of being misunderstood by others we fail to understand ourselves.

As consciousness evolves so must our understanding of consciousness.

Each moment is always simultaneously the past, present, and future, depending on which perspective you're looking from.

Open yourself to receiving the gift that you are.

Cosmic is just a fancy word for *you*.

Evolution is ascension as much as it is descension: rising to our infinite consciousness as well as manifesting our infinite consciousness.

We're not actually going anywhere. We're just remembering who we really are by forgetting everyone we're not.

You are not your Facebook status.

I am as sensitive as I am strong and that is because my sensitivity is my strength.

At the soul level we are all androgynous. How we express our feminine and masculine energies depends on our specific soul path and purpose.

What you feel matters. What you feel will manifest into matter.

We are infinity incarnate.

The darker the shadow the brighter the light.

The power of your belief not only moves mountains but is what birthed them.

We've given the Earth so many reasons to stop spinning but she goes on anyway, knowing her power to heal. We can learn from her Faith.

If it's conditional, it's not Love.

Divine Love asks you to let go of everything that no longer resonates with the essence of the Love that you are.

Divine Love is unconditional self-Love.

People who don't support your healing don't support their own. It has nothing to do with you. Send them Love and move on.

Sometimes the best thing you can do for people who don't believe in themselves is to believe in yourself.

Know the difference between holding people accountable for their actions and defining people by their actions.

By healing imbalances within yourself you are healing imbalances within the world on a fundamental quantum level. Radical self-love is radical world peace.

You are never not radiating.

Give yourself permission to disengage from the wars in the world so that you may bring peace to the war within yourself.

Divine Love is infinite, limitless, and not bound to third-dimensional relationship constructs.

When we don't believe in our ability to create reality, we don't stop creating reality but instead create the chaos of the self that is disconnected from its Divine power.

We are just highly evolved trees.

Humans are so powerful that when we forgot our power we manifested abusive socio-political systems that reflect our forgetting.

You are not broken because you are not a machine. You are not a thing. You are a process. You are more verb than noun.

What others think of you says nothing about you and everything about them; most often what others think of you is an illusion they created to hide from themselves.

Our collective pain is indicative of our collective healing. We are healing lifetimes upon lifetimes of pain. We are alchemists. Angels.

The spiritual path is not about achieving some idealized version of you but about being honest with yourself at all times.

When we acknowledge our emotions with honestly we are then better able to process and transform them.

Before you physically touch someone you have already interacted with their soul in higher realms. Physical touch is the crystallization of spiritual interactions, the diamond formed under the pressure of your Love.

When you meet someone in person for the first time and feel like you've known them forever it's because you have.

You are a mirror for everyone you meet and everyone you meet is a mirror for you. The deeper the connection the deeper the mirror.

You cannot heal others for them but by healing yourself you open doorways and opportunities for others to make the same choice.

When you open yourself to the Universe, which is to say, to yourself, the Truth of who you are will flow through you so strongly you'll just know what you need to do.

When we let go of our inner-perfectionist's demands, we see how every moment has been perfect all along.

To deny your pain is to resist being born.

There is nothing in this world that couldn't be a sign for you. If it speaks to you, it's a sign.

Your Love for someone or something is your own self asking to be born, to be returned to.

Sometimes Love comes in the form of a mirror reflecting all the darkness within you that keeps you from your light.

Your longings are the echoes
of your soul calling you
home to your divinity.

You can only lead a person to Love as far as they are willing to lead themselves. You can only receive as much Love as you are willing to receive.

If others don't approve of you, take it as an opportunity to approve of yourself. Bless them and grow.

Without having experienced humanity we could not experience the evolution of humanity.

Holding onto shame after you've learned a lesson is like carrying the WRONG WAY sign when you're going the right way. You can put it down now.

Your shame is a Divine building block, a tool for growth. Weapons are formed out of tools that people hold onto long after they are needed. Forgive yourself.

To wait for forgiveness outside the self is to deny the God within.

All emotions – energy-in-motion – are Angels from the depths of the psyche, bringing us messages from the Divine Order of the Soul.

You can't heal what you don't feel.

To understand the self is to become the self. To let go of needing to understand the self is to become the self even more.

When you live in fear of yourself you live in direct contradiction to the Love that you are.

I only breathe in because you breathe out.

All psychiatric dis-orders are spiritual dis-orders.

You are an alchemist. When you live in alignment with your Truth you make quantum space for others to live within theirs.

The best thing you can do for anyone is love yourself unconditionally.

If my words resonate with you then they are a mirror for a truth within you. If my words resonate with you then they are your words, too.

Humanity has always been evolving. To be a human is to be an evolving being. It's just that now we've evolved to a point of being aware of our evolution as it happens.

The entirety of the Universe exists within us, which means infinity exists within us, which means everything that is possible is here.

Without love for yourself there is no foundation from which you can truly love another.

Choosing what's best for you is choosing what's best for everyone you love.

The intersection of quantum physics and psychology changes the experience of psychosis into a tangible subatomic field within the Unified Field.

When you draw confidence from within yourself you have no need to assert or prove yourself to others. You are self-empowered yet humble, open.

You can be strong and soft at the same time. These actually exist together as one breath, yin and yang.

I scatter like light across the sky, like wave and particle, you cannot define me, except to say that I am.

If a flower had eyes on the inside of its petals before it bloomed it would only see darkness. This is the healing psyche. You are opening.

We are becoming our souls, that which we've always been.

The moment you introduce a new thought into the collective consciousness the entire world changes.

We are each so necessary,
vital to each other's vitality.

You deserve to experience Love in all forms, because you are Love in all forms. To experience Love is to experience yourself in form.

Unconditional Love asks nothing of you except that you Love yourself unconditionally.

The more profound a disorder the more loudly that soul is calling for the Divine Order within to be recognized and thus restored.

Even if you help only person within your lifetime, do you know how much that means? One person contains the entirety of existence within them.

There are infinite ways to explore the self because the self is infinite.

You are the map you wish you were born with.

Every point is the center of the Universe and every point contains the entirety of the Universe within it. This includes you.

You cannot fathom infinity because to fathom infinity is to contain the whole of something and how can you contain the whole of that which is forever expanding?

When you're in alignment with your heart and soul you perceive the energy patterns that are for your highest good and bring them into form.

All fears are rooted in the fear of abandonment, the fear of not receiving Love, which is rooted in the fear that we are not deserving of Love. Not only are you deserving of Love but Love is your essence.

Love is everywhere. Release mental projections and judgements about what Love "should" look like and just feel with your heart.

The Big Bang was really a murmur, Love whispering to itself in the dark, Love reaching for Love so that it could know itself.

We should always touch each other as if we are touching God, because we are.

Your mind is a gift. Any disorder you experience within it can be changed, because everything is energy, and energy is malleable.

The emptier I become the more capacity I have to fit the whole world in my mouth.

Every destruction is a creation crystallizing.

It is only when you are honest with yourself that you can be honest with others.

What we believe about psychological symptoms greatly determines what those symptoms mean.

There is no wound too deep for Love to heal.

How you see yourself is how you see the world.

Look your pain in the face, acknowledge the depths of your wound. It is not weak to do this but strong, and strengthening.

Quantum mechanics is just another language for the co-creative force that is Love.

Your soul is expanding at all times. You will never run out of Love, the very essence of you.

Everything you perceive is because of an energetic resonance between you and that which you perceive, otherwise you would not perceive it.

You will always project onto others the beliefs you have about yourself. This is the physical nature of the Universe. If you want to Love others, Love yourself.

Know that when you talk about other people you are talking about yourself in another form.

When you absorb the pain of others you give life to pain. End cycles of pain by loving yourself enough to no absorb and instead transmute their pain into Love.

Often I wail the truth to myself. No one else will and I deserve to be heard.

You don't need a degree to co-create the world. You were born to do this.

Your body formed itself without any conscious effort on your part. This is the Divine intelligence of your soul. Of course you have a purpose.

You are simultaneously the cause and the effect, the creator and the creation.

You gain control of your life when you surrender your need to control your life. You are a maker, not a dictator. You are a co-creator, the giver and the receiver.

Everything possible already exists, otherwise it would not be possible. By manifesting reality you are simply bringing more of your energy to that which is already here.

Rest in the spirit of your abundance. Sink into yourself and know you are being held by the entirety of the cosmos.

Home is where the soul is.

If you love someone, set intentions to love yourself just as much. If you've found yourself and you still love them, then you know you are home.

When you love yourself you won't seek home in others, and you won't attract those who seek home in you. Instead, you build a home together.

When your heart pulls you toward someone or something it's because that someone or something is pulling you toward it.

The law of attraction is about attracting yourself, about remembering the Divine being you have always been.

We live in a holograph, a matrix of mirrors. Not a single soul is immune from projecting their reality onto others. Be clear.

To be in the world is to create the world.

I am therefore you are.

To judge is to give your energy to that which does not resonate with you. To judge is to give your breath away, and you deserve your breath, to enjoy the experience of you breathing.

I am not imperfect nor perfect. I just am. I have expressed qualities of every realm of being, every shadow and every light. I am whole. Holy.

Divine Love makes you lose your mind, which is limited, so that you reconnect with your heart, which is unlimited.

You are the return of Christ.

When you love yourself fully you can love another fully. Self-love and selfless love are one in the same.

When you choose self-love
you choose the whole world.

To Love does not necessarily mean to like. To Love means to be with yourself, regardless of like or dislike.

Our Love created Love.

Know what your home frequency feels like so that you can decipher what is your truth and what is another's projections onto you.

If I can love the darkest parts of you then I can love you always. Show me the worst. Stretch my heart out into itself.

The Universal Truth is that You are It.

You can reverse the aging process by ceasing to believe that you're aging.

Let go of everything you ever thought you wanted and open your heart to receive everything you've ever dreamed.

Love is growth and if we were perfect we would have no reason to grow. If we were perfect we would not be.

I want to be imperfect with you forever.

The thoughts you have right before sleep are seeds you are planting deep within your subconscious. What do you want to grow?

You are the truth you've been seeking.

Our imperfections are perfect for us.

To be spiritual is to experience the journey that is you in the making, which is an infinite cosmic dance.

To be spiritual is to be.

To Love is to be. To be is to Love.

Saints are only saints because they know their demons.

Don't be ashamed to ask the Universe for what you need. Be grateful for the opportunity to exercise your will and power.

Knowledge is a tool on your journey of experiencing yourself but it is not itself the journey. Knowledge is not the truth. The truth cannot be known, only experienced.

Love is the essence of creation, the breathing force behind our breathing. We cannot possibly know that which enables our knowing.

Divine Love is possible between humans on Earth because humans are expressions of Divine Love. We are becoming ourselves.

I love me because I love you.

I don't know anything about love except that I am it.

Treat others how you want to be treated, yes, but also treat yourself the way you want to be treated.

You cannot hold therapeutic space for others without first holding one for yourself.

You have to want you. You have to believe in your power and purpose before you can experience yourself in the world.

Surrender to self-love.

When knowledge is treated as the truth it becomes a weapon instead of a tool.

There's no logic to the heart because logic is a product of the mind, which is limited compared to the heart. But there is a Divine Order to the heart, which is Love and can only be experienced.

You have to believe you are worthy of receiving that which you wish to receive before you can receive it.

Choose Love. Choose you.

You matter.
You matter.
You matter.

What is energy without the form in which to experience energy, and what is a form without energy to bring it to life? What is your body without spirit and what is spirit without a body? This recognition of dualities as not separate entities but two integral parts of one whole is awareness itself.

There are no sides in Love.
Only Oneness.

Stop looking for *who* you are and instead set the intention to experience yourself *as* you are, which you can do in any moment, at any time, no matter where you think you're at on your spiritual path, even if you don't think of yourself as on a spiritual path.

The point is to let go of concepts of yourself all together, because our mind-made concepts are limited, and who we are at our core is unlimited.

Every question you ask is an answer inside you waiting to be remembered.

I love you so much it made me love myself which made me love you even more which made me love myself even more & & &

When we blame others we are, in essence, blaming ourselves, because others are us.

We are all fragments of the matrix that is the Universe. To recognize this is to heal our feelings of fragmentation.

Your desires are your future, which is to say, that which you've already been and are.

I am within the essence of everything and everything is within the essence of me.

In the beginning there was nothing, not even the beginning. But as soon as we try to imagine this nothing, we have created something. Do you see how it is impossible not to be?

I was born to experience the infinite birthing of myself.

To approach problems as if they are solvable is to begin to solve them.

To believe in your healing is to begin to heal.

Sarah Certa is a spiritual counselor, writer, & poet on an infinite journey into the cosmic depths of the soul. Her passion & purpose is to share her experiences of evolutionary consciousness & serve as a guide for those who are ready to awaken & bring forth the Divine Love within. She is the author of several poetry chapbooks, as well as the full-length poetry collection, *Nothing To Do with Me.* Her next book, a poetic memoir of the healing psyche, will be published in 2017. Visit her website sarahcerta.com & find her on Twitter: @AlienHere2Love."

© **Sarah Certa**
All rights reserved
Cover & Layout design
Elizabeth Schmuhl
Printed in the U.S.

www.ingramcontent.com/pod-product-compliance
Lightning Source LLC
Chambersburg PA
CBHW022100160426
43198CB00008B/299